Was **Muhammad** (pbuh)
Really a Christian?

ISBN: 9798346607366

Was Muhammad really a Christian?

Solar Prime Supreme:131: Lazarus Lamel

Chapter 1: The Early Context of Christianity and Islam
In this chapter, we journey back to the 6th and 7th centuries in Arabia, where the region's spiritual diversity created a fertile ground for new ideas. This environment, with its Jewish, Christian, and other monotheistic influences, provided **Muhammad** with a foundation that would shape the core of his message. We explore the historical context that set the stage for Islam and examine how the ethical teachings of Jesus and other monotheistic values permeated Arabian society.

Chapter 2: The Teachings of Jesus and the Moral Code of Islam
Here, we compare the moral teachings of Jesus with the ethical framework of Islam. We delve into principles shared by both figures—such as humility, charity, forgiveness, and compassion—and how these values became central to both **Christianity** and Islam. We'll see how **Muhammad**'s emphasis on social justice, charity, and reverence for God aligns closely with Jesus' teachings.

Chapter 3: The Role of Jesus in the Quran
This chapter examines how Jesus is honored in the **Quran** as a prophet, healer, and righteous guide. We explore the reverence Islam holds for Jesus and his mother, Mary, as well as the stories in the **Quran** that emphasize Jesus' moral integrity and spiritual significance. Through these passages, we uncover the shared respect for Jesus that both Islam and **Christianity** hold.

Chapter 4: Muhammad's Perspective on the Crucifixion
Islam's interpretation of the crucifixion contrasts with the traditional Christian narrative. Here, we explore the **Quran**'s assertion that Jesus was not crucified, reflecting a divine protection of his honor. We discuss how **Muhammad**'s perspective on Jesus' mission upholds his legacy while affirming Islam's monotheistic principles, offering a view that honors Jesus' message without adopting the crucifixion as central.

Chapter 5: Muhammad's Relationship with Khadijah and Waraqah: The Christian Influence
In this chapter, we dive into the intimate support system that shaped **Muhammad**'s early years as a prophet. Khadijah, a devout Christian, and her uncle, Waraqah, a scholar of the Torah and Gospels, influenced **Muhammad** deeply. Their support, faith, and moral values contributed to his understanding of monotheism, justice, and compassion. We explore how

their influence intertwined with his mission, laying a foundation for his message.

Chapter 6: Historical Interactions between Christians and Muslims

This chapter highlights the early alliances and respectful interactions between Muslims and Christians. From the migration to Abyssinia to diplomatic relations with Christian tribes, we explore how **Muhammad** and his followers formed connections with Christian communities. These relationships set a precedent of tolerance, diplomacy, and mutual respect, revealing the potential for unity between the two faiths.

Chapter 7: Influence of Popes and Rulers on the Development of Islam

Here, we examine how Christian leaders and scholars indirectly influenced Islam. From Byzantine emperors to the intellectual exchanges with Christian scholars, we see how interactions between Muslims and Christians shaped the development of Islamic thought. The chapter sheds light on how political and theological encounters contributed to the cross-pollination of ideas that enriched both traditions.

Chapter 8: The Spread of Islam and the Message of Jesus

In this chapter, we explore how Islam's teachings of compassion, social justice, and charity resonated with Christian communities as the faith spread across regions. We examine how Islamic governance provided religious tolerance and mutual respect, allowing Islam to expand peacefully in areas populated by Christians. This chapter reveals the ethical kinship that helped bridge the two faiths.

Conclusion: Reexamining the Legacy of Muhammad as a Christ-Like Figure

In the conclusion, we reflect on **Muhammad**'s life through the lens of his Christ-like qualities. We explore how his dedication to humility, justice, and monotheism presents him as a figure aligned with Jesus' teachings. This chapter reaffirms the shared values and ethical connections between Islam and **Christianity**, inviting readers to see **Muhammad**'s legacy as a continuation of Jesus' call for compassion, unity, and reverence for God.

Master Key Application #157
Codex 4

Introduction

Qhum, Salutations to the Primes! 747-24-7-361*

Messiahs, Emperors, Queens, and Kings—within these pages, I invite you to a journey that will pull back layers of history, challenging what you thought you knew about the Prophet **Muhammad** and his connection to the teachings of Asar/Heru/Yashua also known as

Jesus. *Was **Muhammad** Really a Christian?* is not merely a question; it's an investigation into two legacies that echo across centuries, two figures whose teachings might share far more than what we've been led to believe.

Imagine **Muhammad** in his early days, supported and inspired by his devout Christian wife, Khadijah, and her learned uncle, Waraqah, a man who memorized the Torah and the Gospels. Khadijah believed in **Muhammad**'s calling and invested everything she had—her wealth, faith, and energy—to support him. Together, their commitment shaped a message that emphasized compassion, humility, and justice, values deeply resonant with the teachings of Jesus. Could it be that **Muhammad**'s vision was inspired not to oppose, but to uphold the spirit of Jesus' teachings?

This book will take you from the words of the **Quran** to the stories of the Bible, exploring the way Jesus is honored in Islam as a prophet, a healer, a guide—qualities celebrated in both faiths. You'll see how **Muhammad** called for charity, humility, and forgiveness, values at the heart of Jesus' message. And you'll witness the respect and alliances **Muhammad** cultivated with Christian tribes and leaders, not as mere political gestures, but as a profound acknowledgment of shared beliefs.

In each chapter, we'll delve into the intersections of **Christianity** and Islam, where mutual respect and moral kinship are evident. We'll journey through **Muhammad**'s early days, guided by Khadijah's faith and Waraqah's wisdom, to the **Quran**'s reverence for Jesus and Mary, and finally, to the influence of Christian leaders and scholars on Islam's development. Along the way, we'll encounter the treaties, alliances, and messages exchanged between Christian and Muslim communities—revealing moments of harmony that defy the divisions imposed by history.

This is not a story of diluted doctrines but a powerful narrative of connected paths—each retaining its own distinct voice yet resonating with shared values of love, justice, and reverence for God. As we uncover these connections, I invite you to see **Muhammad** not as an opposition to Jesus, but perhaps as a kindred spirit, a Christ-like figure in his own right, calling humanity to unity, compassion, and faith. You may find that Islam and **Christianity** are not separate visions, but reflections of the same call—to live a life rooted in humility, integrity, and the worship of the One True God.

Arabic Alphabet Syntax

Letter (Isolated)		Transliteration	Name (Arabic)	Forms
أ	ʾ (a)	Alif	Isolated: أ, Initial: أ, Medial: ـا, Final: ـا
ب	b	Bāʾ	Isolated: ب, Initial: بـ, Medial: ـبـ, Final: ـب
ت	t	Tāʾ	Isolated: ت, Initial: تـ, Medial: ـتـ, Final: ـت
ث	th	Thāʾ	Isolated: ث, Initial: ثـ, Medial: ـثـ, Final: ـث
ج	j	Jīm	Isolated: ج, Initial: جـ, Medial: ـجـ, Final: ـج
ح	ḥ	Ḥāʾ	Isolated: ح, Initial: حـ, Medial: ـحـ, Final: ـح
خ	kh	Khāʾ	Isolated: خ, Initial: خـ, Medial: ـخـ, Final: ـخ
د	d	Dāl	Isolated: د, Initial: د, Medial: ـد, Final: ـد
ذ	dh	Dhāl	Isolated: ذ, Initial: ذ, Medial: ـذ, Final: ـذ
ر	r	Rāʾ	Isolated: ر, Initial: ر, Medial: ـر, Final: ـر
ز	z	Zāy	Isolated: ز, Initial: ز, Medial: ـز, Final: ـز
س	s	Sīn	Isolated: س, Initial: سـ, Medial: ـسـ, Final: ـس
ش	sh	Shīn	Isolated: ش, Initial: شـ, Medial: ـشـ, Final: ـش
ص	ṣ	Ṣād	Isolated: ص, Initial: صـ, Medial: ـصـ, Final: ـص
ض	ḍ	Ḍād	Isolated: ض, Initial: ضـ, Medial: ـضـ, Final: ـض
ط	ṭ	Ṭāʾ	Isolated: ط, Initial: طـ, Medial: ـطـ, Final: ـط
ظ	ẓ	Ẓāʾ	Isolated: ظ, Initial: ظـ, Medial: ـظـ, Final: ـظ
ع	ʿ	ʿAyn	Isolated: ع, Initial: عـ, Medial: ـعـ, Final: ـع
غ	gh	Ghayn	Isolated: غ, Initial: غـ, Medial: ـغـ, Final: ـغ
ف	f	Fāʾ	Isolated: ف, Initial: فـ, Medial: ـف, Final: ـف

ق	q	Qāf	Isolated: ق, Initial: ‑ قـ, Medial: ‑ قـ ‑, Final: ‑ق
ك	k	Kāf	Isolated: ك, Initial: ‑ کـ, Medial: ‑ کـ ‑, Final: ‑ك
ل	l	Lām	Isolated: ل, Initial: ‑ لـ, Medial: ‑ لـ ‑, Final: ‑ل
م	m	Mīm	Isolated: م, Initial: ‑ مـ, Medial: ‑ مـ ‑, Final: ‑م
ن	n	Nūn	Isolated: ن, Initial: ‑ نـ, Medial: ‑ نـ ‑, Final: ‑ن
ه	h	Hāʾ	Isolated: ه, Initial: هـ, Medial: ‑ هـ, Final: ‑ه
و	w	Wāw	Isolated: و, Initial: و, Medial: ‑و, Final: ‑و
ي	y	Yāʾ	Isolated: ي, Initial: ‑ يـ, Medial: ‑ يـ ‑, Final: ‑ي

Chapter 1:
The Early Context of Christianity and Islam

Chapter 1: The Early Context of Christianity and Islam

:1 Greetings, Messiahs. As we begin this journey into the life and teachings of the Prophet **Muhammad**, walk with me back through time to the **6**th century, to the deserts and cities of the Arabian Peninsula. This was a land marked by ancient routes, connecting empires, faiths, and cultures, shaping a world on the edge of transformation.

:2 Around **570** AD, **Muhammad** was born in **Mecca**—a city that lay along the trade routes linking the **Byzantine Empire** to the north, the Sassanian (Persian) Empire to the east, and the Christian kingdom of Aksum across the Red Sea.

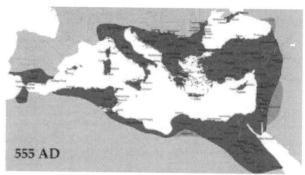

555 AD

Positioned as a crossroads, **Mecca** became a melting pot where merchants and travelers brought not only goods but also ideas, beliefs, and spiritual practices.

:3 Mecca, surrounded by the vast **Hijaz desert**, thrived with life and culture despite the arid landscape. Its people made pilgrimages to the Kaaba (ﺍﻟ ﻛ ﻌ ﺑﺔ), a sacred sanctuary that housed idols worshipped by various tribes, but also held the idea of a central place of reverence—a unity **Muhammad** would later reshape.

:4 Yet, by **Muhammad**'s time, monotheistic beliefs had already begun to influence Arabia. Jewish, Christian, and even Zoroastrian (from Persia) communities had settled in pockets throughout the region, providing glimpses into the idea of one God—an idea that would shape **Muhammad**'s own understanding.

:5 Christianity reached Arabia primarily through two avenues: trade and missionary work. As early as the **5**th century, Christian missionaries from the Ethiopian kingdom of Aksum were active in Yemen, establishing communities and spreading teachings. Around **525** AD, the Aksumite king Kaleb had intervened militarily to protect Christians in the region from persecution.

:6 In **Yemen** and **Najran** to the south, the **Ethiopian** Christians formed thriving communities, bringing with them the stories of Jesus (عيسى) and Mary (مريم). This Christian influence would be significant, as **Muhammad** would later encounter these figures in the monotheistic vision he shared.

:7 North of the Arabian Peninsula, the **Byzantine Empire**, with **Christianity** as its official religion, wielded considerable influence. The **Ghassanids**, a Christian Arab tribe allied with **Byzantium**, guarded the empire's frontier, spreading Christian teachings throughout northern Arabia.

:8 In the early **600**s, the long and exhausting wars between the Byzantine and Sassanian empires disrupted trade and created uncertainty. This era, ripe with turmoil and change, set the stage for a new spiritual movement—a movement that would rise in the Arabian desert.

:9 By the time **Muhammad** reached adulthood around **600** AD, Arabia was already a place where Jews, Christians, and Zoroastrians interacted alongside the indigenous polytheistic tribes. Each group brought with it a unique understanding of the divine, enriching **Muhammad**'s exposure to different expressions of faith.

:**10** Jewish tribes in cities like **Yathrib** (يَثْرِب), later renamed **Medina** (المَدِينَة), practiced a strict monotheism honoring prophets like Abraham (إِبْرَاهِيم) and Moses (مُوسَى). This adherence to one God and moral law would later resonate in **Muhammad**'s teachings.

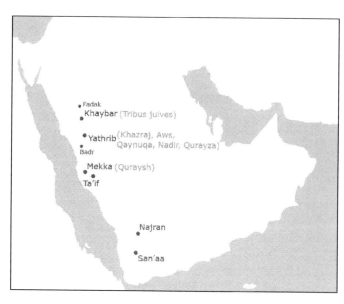

:**11 Christianity**, however, was not a unified belief. Arabian Christians came from different sects: Nestorians, **Monophysites**, and others, each with their own view of Jesus. Some emphasized his human nature; others, his divine essence. These differing interpretations provided alternative perspectives that **Muhammad** would likely encounter.

:**12** The Nestorians, for instance, focused on Jesus as a human prophet, a teacher without the divine status afforded him in Byzantine orthodoxy. This viewpoint aligned closely with **Muhammad**'s later reverence for Jesus as a prophet, rather than as God.

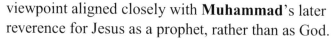

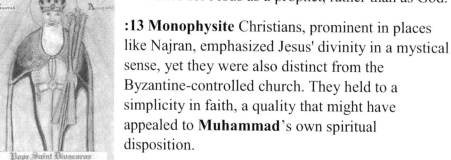

:**13 Monophysite** Christians, prominent in places like Najran, emphasized Jesus' divinity in a mystical sense, yet they were also distinct from the Byzantine-controlled church. They held to a simplicity in faith, a quality that might have appealed to **Muhammad**'s own spiritual disposition.

:**14** Living in **Mecca**, **Muhammad** would have encountered these teachings and stories from traders, monks, and travelers alike. Values of compassion, humility, and devotion to one God were messages shared among Christians and Jews, themes that would emerge in **Muhammad**'s later life.

:15 By the early **600**s, *Najran's Christian* community was established, with its own churches, bishops, and organized religious life. This community was strong in the years leading to **Muhammad**'s first revelations in **610** AD, a time when he was likely exposed to Christian teachings.

:16 The Kaaba, though filled with idols, was a center of pilgrimage for many tribes, and its unifying significance was apparent even in pre-Islamic Arabia. **Muhammad** would later use this concept of unity, transforming it into a place for the worship of one God alone.

:17 Monotheism, while not dominant in **Mecca**, was a concept **Muhammad** saw practiced by his Jewish and Christian contemporaries. His prophetic message would ultimately call the people to this same singular devotion.

:18 When **Muhammad** began preaching, he upheld values found in Jewish and Christian teachings: justice, humility, and compassion. These core ideals, present in the monotheistic faiths around him, would shape Islam's ethical structure.

:19 Almsgiving, which **Muhammad** would institutionalize as **zakat** (الزكاة), paralleled the Christian concept of charity and the Jewish practice of tzedakah. Through zakat, **Muhammad** extended the principle of caring for the community, a theme close to the teachings of Jesus.

:20 Consider, Messiahs, how **Muhammad**'s early exposure to these monotheistic faiths provided him with a framework for a divine covenant. It's no coincidence that Islam shares such strong ethical ties with its sister Abrahamic religions.

ST. ARETHAS AND COMPANIONS, MARTYRS

:21 Around **613** AD, when **Muhammad** began preaching openly in **Mecca**, his message echoed the call of previous prophets to turn from idol worship and embrace a moral life. This was a call familiar to the Christian and Jewish communities of his time.

:22 In his encounters, **Muhammad** met individuals who recognized something special in him. A Christian monk, Bahira, is said to have recognized **Muhammad**'s potential, believing him to carry the qualities of an ancient prophet.

:23 When persecution intensified, **Muhammad** instructed some followers to seek refuge with the Christian king of Abyssinia in **615** AD. The Negus, known for his kindness, gave them sanctuary, demonstrating a shared respect between **Muhammad** and the Christian community.

:24 Islam's reverence for Jesus and Mary within the **Quran** reflects **Muhammad**'s awareness and respect for these figures. Jesus is honored not as God, but as a prophet, a healer, and a guide—a teacher of compassion and wisdom.

:25 Over two decades of revelations, the **Quran** presented a Jesus who was righteous and compassionate, emphasizing moral conduct and purity— qualities that reflect the reverence Christians held for him.

:26 By **622** AD, when **Muhammad**
migrated to **Medina**, he was carrying a
vision of community built on faith,
compassion, and justice. The Jewish
tribes there welcomed him, recognizing
in his message the echoes of their own
beliefs.

:27 In **Medina**, **Muhammad**'s teachings
would further develop, drawing from the
Jewish and Christian ideas he
encountered. These influences shaped a
broader narrative that would establish Islam as a continuation of the
Abrahamic tradition.

:28 The **Quran**'s respect for Jesus and Mary demonstrated a connection to
Christian values, as **Muhammad** honored Jesus' moral message while
clarifying Islam's strict monotheism.

:29 When **Muhammad** returned to **Mecca** in **630** AD, he purified the
Kaaba, rededicating it to the one God. This act symbolized the culmination
of his monotheistic mission, echoing the values he had witnessed among
Christians and Jews.

:30 Emperors and empresses, **Muhammad**'s message was built on the
moral ideals of compassion, humility, and charity—echoes of Jesus'
teachings, redefined for his people and his time.

:31 By the end of his life in **632** AD, **Muhammad** had forged a new path
for his people, drawing from the spiritual traditions he encountered. His
message, grounded in the timeless ethics of the prophets before him, would
continue to resonate, carrying forward the principles of faith, compassion,
and unity for future generations.

Chapter 2:
The Teachings of Jesus and the Moral Code of Islam

Chapter 2: The Teachings of Jesus and the Moral Code of Islam

:1 Messiahs, as we delve into this chapter, I invite you to see the shared values and teachings between Jesus and **Muhammad**. These moral principles are not only parallel but often mirror one another in depth and spirit. I will provide both biblical and **Quran**ic references, complete with dates of revelation, to ground these parallels in time and scripture.

:2 Let's begin with Jesus' teaching on love, compassion, and humility. Around **30** AD, in the Sermon on the Mount, Jesus spoke of compassion as the core of moral life, famously saying, *"Blessed are the meek, for they shall inherit the earth"* (Matthew **5:5**). This call for humility resonates deeply within Islam as well.

:3 Around **610** AD, when **Muhammad** received his first revelations in **Mecca**, the **Quran** began to instill a similar virtue of humility before God (الله   ). In one early revelation, God tells believers, *"And do not turn your face away from people with pride, nor walk haughtily on the earth"* (**Quran 31:18**). This guidance, revealed in the early years of Islam, reflects a humility that mirrors Jesus' teachings.

:4 Charity is another central value. In the book of Matthew, written between **80–90** AD, Jesus advises a rich man to give to the poor, saying, *"If you want to be perfect, go, sell your possessions and give to the poor"* (Matthew **19:21**). This principle of charity as a path to righteousness is also emphasized in the **Quran**.

:5 In **622** AD, the **Quran**ic injunction for zakat (زكاة), or almsgiving, was established in **Medina** as one of the *Five Pillars of Islam*. The **Quran** declares, *"Take from their wealth a charity by which you purify them and cause them to increase"* (**Quran 9:103**). Zakat became a mandatory act, emphasizing the same spirit of selflessness and care for the needy that Jesus taught.

:6 The theme of forgiveness is also central to both teachings. Jesus, around **30** AD, was asked how often one should forgive, to which he responded, *"Not seven times, but seventy times seven"* (Matthew **18:22**). This emphasis on boundless forgiveness is echoed in the **Quran**'s view of God's mercy.

:7 In **615** AD, early **Meccan** verses revealed the merciful nature of God, urging believers to forgive one another. *"And let them pardon and overlook. Would you not like that Allah should forgive you?"* (**Quran 24:22**). This directive aligns with Jesus' teaching, reinforcing a moral framework of forgiveness.

:8 Jesus' famous teaching on judgment—*"Do not judge, or you too will be judged"* (Matthew **7:1**), written around **80–90** AD—warns against self-righteousness. Islam, too, emphasizes that only God can judge the hearts and intentions of individuals, and **Muhammad** cautioned against arrogance and judgment.

:9 In the early years of Islam, around **614** AD, the **Quran** advised, *"Do not spy, nor backbite one another"* (**Quran 49:12**), underscoring a code of respect and restraint from judgment. This parallels Jesus' call for empathy and a humble approach to one's own fallibility.

:10 Both Jesus and **Muhammad** upheld patience, particularly in adversity. Jesus taught endurance, counseling his followers to trust in God's will. Around **30** AD, he exemplified this in his response to hardship and opposition.

:11 The **Quran**, in a revelation from **616** AD, emphasizes patience as a virtue of the faithful: *"And be patient, for indeed, Allah does not allow to be* *lost the reward of those who do good"* (**Quran 11:115**). **Muhammad** encouraged his followers to endure with trust, embodying the same virtue Jesus taught.

:12 Jesus warned against the dangers of greed. In Matthew, written around **80–90** AD, he says, *"You cannot serve both God and money"* (Matthew **6:24**). **Muhammad** echoed this caution, discouraging attachment to wealth.

:13 In the year **624** AD, the **Quran** advised balance and moderation: *"And those who, when they spend, are neither extravagant nor stingy, but hold a just balance between those extremes"* (**Quran 25:67**). This call to avoid excessive materialism reflects Jesus' concern for spiritual priorities.

:14 Justice, especially for the marginalized, was another core value for Jesus. He spoke against the oppression of the weak, urging compassion and equity. Around **30** AD, he challenged societal norms, advocating for the voiceless and downtrodden.

:15 Similarly, justice (عدل) is a fundamental principle in Islam. In **622** AD, the **Quran** declared, *"O you who believe, be persistently standing firm in justice, witnesses for Allah"* (**Quran 4:135**). This passage aligns with Jesus' own call for social justice, emphasizing equity for all.

:16 Love is perhaps the most profound message both figures preached. Jesus, around **30** AD, declared love to be the greatest commandment: *"Love the Lord your God... and love your neighbor as yourself"* (Matthew **22:37-40**).

:17 **Muhammad**'s teachings echo this love for God and humanity. In **630** AD, the **Quran** revealed, *"And lower your wing to the believers who follow you"* (**Quran 26:215**). This call to treat others with kindness reflects Jesus' own principle of love and compassion.

:18 Prayer was central to both Jesus' and **Muhammad**'s lives. Jesus would withdraw to pray, modeling devotion. The Gospels, written decades later, emphasize Jesus' connection with God through prayer.

:19 Around **610** AD, the importance of prayer (صلاة) was revealed to **Muhammad** in **Mecca**, establishing it as a pillar of Islam. "Establish prayer to remember Me," God says in **Quran 20:14**. This ritual of connection mirrors Jesus' own dedication to prayer.

:20 Fasting as self-discipline is another shared practice. Jesus fasted for *40 days*, an act of devotion and focus. This practice of fasting is significant in both traditions.

:21 In **624** AD, the observance of Ramadan (رمضان) became obligatory for Muslims, signifying self-restraint and renewal. The **Quran** states, *"O you who have believed, decreed upon you is fasting... that you may become righteous"* (**Quran 2:183**). This act of devotion reflects Jesus' practice of fasting.

:22 The sanctity of life is a principle Jesus often preached, associating kindness with godliness. Around **30** AD, his compassion for all life was a hallmark of his teachings.

:23 Islam holds life as sacred. The **Quran**, in a revelation from **625** AD, equates taking an innocent life with killing all of humanity: *"Whoever kills a soul... it is as if he had slain mankind entirely"* (**Quran 5:32**). This principle mirrors the reverence for life Jesus imparted.

:24 Jesus often acted as a healer, caring for the sick. **Muhammad**'s teachings also advocated for the care of the vulnerable, including the sick and elderly.

:25 Both leaders warned against hypocrisy. Jesus admonished the Pharisees for their outward piety. **Muhammad** similarly warned against empty displays of faith, emphasizing sincerity.

:26 Jesus taught that one's treasure should be in heaven, not on earth (Matthew **6:20**). **Muhammad** reminded believers that true wealth lies in faith and good deeds.

:27 Family and community respect were upheld by both. Jesus emphasized family bonds, and **Muhammad** taught the duty to honor one's parents, especially mothers.

:28 Service to others is a shared value. Jesus washed his disciples' feet, a gesture of humility. **Muhammad** taught that "the best among you are those who benefit others."

:29 Humility is a cornerstone of both teachings. Jesus' message exalted the humble, and **Muhammad** warned against arrogance.

:30 Through these principles, **Muhammad** brought forward a vision of life that mirrored Jesus' teachings, grounded in moral integrity and compassion.

:31 These parallels show that Islam preserved the moral core of Jesus' teachings, revealing that these two faiths, while distinct, share a foundation of universal values in humility, justice, and love.

Chapter 3:
The Role of Jesus in the Quran

Chapter 3: The Role of Jesus in the Quran

:1 Messiahs, let us now examine how Jesus (عيسى) is portrayed within the **Quran**. The **Quran**, revealed to **Muhammad** over a span of **23** years from **610** to **632** AD, speaks of Jesus with a reverence and respect that demonstrates his significance within Islam. Unlike the traditional Christian view of Jesus as divine, Islam sees him as a revered prophet, one of the greatest messengers of God. Let us delve into these revelations, exploring how the **Quran** elevates Jesus' message in ways that align with the moral codes and prophetic traditions he established.

:2 The **Quran** references Jesus nearly **25** times, and he is called "*Isa ibn Maryam*" (Jesus, son of Mary) throughout, highlighting his unique birth. The emphasis on Jesus as the "son of Mary" not only distinguishes him but also honors his mother, Mary (مريم) (symbolic of the holy Mother), who is given a prominent role in the **Quran**.

:3 Mary herself is the only woman mentioned by name in the **Quran**, and a full chapter, Surah Maryam (سورة مريم), or Chapter **19**, is dedicated to her. This chapter, revealed around **615** AD in **Mecca**, recounts the miraculous birth of Jesus

The Ancient Church of Al-Aqiser

and affirms Mary's purity and righteousness, reflecting an honor given to no other woman in Islamic scripture.

:4 In Surah Maryam, we find the story of Jesus' birth: "*And mention, [O Muhammad], in the Book [the story of] Mary, when she withdrew from her family to a place toward the east*" (**Quran 19:16**). Here, the **Quran** draws parallels to the miraculous birth narrative found in Christian traditions, showing that Jesus' conception was by divine decree.

:5 Mary's experience, described in this revelation from **615** AD, closely mirrors the New Testament accounts of the Annunciation. Both narratives uphold Mary's purity and submission to God's will, and in both traditions, she is a model of piety and faith.

:6 Jesus' first miracle, according to Islamic tradition, occurred while he was still an infant. The **Quran** narrates, "He [Jesus] said, *'Indeed, I am the servant of Allah. He has given me the Scripture and made me a prophet'''* (**Quran 19:30**). This verse from Surah Maryam reflects Jesus' early awareness of his divine mission, a concept that aligns with Christian beliefs about his special role.

:7 Unlike the Christian Gospels, which were written between **50–100** AD, the **Quran**ic revelation emphasizes Jesus as a human prophet rather than a divine being. This distinction is significant, as it establishes Jesus firmly within the Islamic framework of prophecy, alongside figures like Moses (مو سى) and Abraham (إب راهيم).

:8 The **Quran** calls Jesus the "Messiah" (ال م س يح), a title that signifies his role as anointed by God. "*The Messiah, Jesus, the son of Mary, was but a messenger of* ***Allah and His word***" (**Quran 4:171**). This verse, revealed in **Medina** around **627** AD, acknowledges Jesus as the

Arab Church in Baghdadiyah District of Jeddah not far from Al-Balad, near Hail and Hamzah Shahatah Streets

Messiah, aligning with Christian terminology while affirming his human nature.

:9 In Islam, Jesus' role as Messiah is interpreted as a figure who brings guidance and hope, not as a savior in the divine sense. This concept respects Jesus' mission while maintaining Islam's strict monotheism, where only God (Allah) is divine.

:10 The **Quran** also refers to Jesus as a "Word" (كلمة) from God, a term that resonates with the Christian concept of the "Word made flesh" in the Gospel of John, written around **90** AD. However, while **Christianity** interprets this as Jesus' divinity, Islam sees it as God's command, through which Jesus was created.

:11 Surah Al-Imran (سورة آل عمران), revealed around **625** AD in **Medina**, speaks of Jesus' miracles, such as healing the blind and the leper, and raising the dead by God's permission. "*And I cure the blind and the leper, and I give life to the dead—by permission of Allah*" (**Quran 3:49**). This aligns with New Testament accounts of Jesus' miracles, though the **Quran** attributes them to God's will.

:12 By attributing Jesus' miracles to God's power, Islam reinforces its monotheistic beliefs while still honoring Jesus' unique role. This recognition of Jesus as a healer and prophet builds a bridge between Islamic and Christian views, emphasizing shared reverence for his moral and spiritual impact.

:13 Another important **Quran**ic reference to Jesus comes in Surah Al-Maidah (سورة المائدة), revealed in **Medina** around **627** AD, which recounts Jesus' interaction with his disciples. He asks for a table from heaven as a sign for them, saying, "*Our Lord, send down to us a table [spread with food] from the heaven to be for us a festival*" (**Quran 5:114**). This mirrors the Christian idea of the Last Supper, connecting Jesus' story across both traditions.

:14 The **Quran** also acknowledges Jesus' role in delivering the Injil (إنجيل), or the Gospel, revealed as a scripture that contains guidance and light. In Surah Al-Maidah, it says, "*And We sent, following in their footsteps, Jesus, the son of Mary, confirming that which came before him in* *the Torah; and We gave him the Gospel"* (**Quran 5:46**). This passage, revealed in **Medina**, aligns with Christian beliefs about Jesus bringing divine teachings.

:15 Unlike the Gospels, written decades after Jesus' life, the **Quran**ic reference to the Injil affirms its status as a revealed scripture rather than a biographical account. Islam sees the Gospel as a continuation of God's message, reflecting Jesus' role as a link in the prophetic chain.

:16 Jesus' teachings of compassion, mercy, and love for one's neighbor are values that the **Quran** upholds. In **625** AD, the **Quran** revealed, *"Indeed, the mercy of Allah is near to the doers of good"* (**Quran 7:56**). This message of mercy echoes Jesus' teachings and solidifies the **Quran**'s call for compassion.

:17 Jesus' role as a prophet of peace is also honored in the **Quran**. He is called a "spirit from God" (منه روح) in Surah An-Nisa (ال ذساء سورة), revealed in **627** AD, which says, *"The Messiah, Jesus, the son of Mary, was... a spirit from Him"* (**Quran 4:171**). This phrase reinforces Jesus' connection to God, while still upholding his human status.

:18 The **Quran**'s depiction of Jesus aligns with his teachings in the New Testament. Around **30** AD, Jesus taught forgiveness and kindness, saying, *"Love your enemies and pray for those who persecute you"* (Matthew **5:44**). The **Quran** shares this ethic, advising believers to *"repel [evil] with what is better"* (**Quran 41:34**).

:19 Islam also upholds the belief in Jesus' return. Muslims believe that Jesus will come again as a sign of the end times, a belief shared by certain Christian traditions. This shared expectation reflects the respect both faiths have for his lasting role in divine history.

:20 In Surah Az-Zukhruf (ال زخرف سورة), revealed around **620** AD, the **Quran** states, *"And indeed, Jesus will be [a sign for] knowledge of the Hour"* (**Quran 43:61**), affirming that his return will herald a significant moment. This belief in Jesus' eschatological role strengthens the continuity between Islamic and Christian perspectives.

:21 The **Quran** honors Jesus as a moral example, teaching love and compassion. In Surah Al-Mumtahanah (الممتحنة سورة), revealed around **630** AD, God says, *"Allah does not forbid you from those who do not fight you because of religion and do not expel you from your homes"* (**Quran 60:8**), reflecting the love and tolerance Jesus exemplified.

:22 While Islam rejects the idea of the crucifixion, it nonetheless respects Jesus' willingness to sacrifice for his faith. Surah An-Nisa, revealed in **627** AD, states, *"They did not kill him, nor did they crucify him; but it was made to appear so to them"* (**Quran 4:157**). This passage underscores Islam's view of Jesus as a dedicated servant of God, even without the crucifixion narrative.

:23 Islamic tradition holds that Jesus was taken up by God, an event Muslims view as his divine protection rather than resurrection. This interpretation preserves Jesus' dignity while aligning with Islamic teachings about God's power to save.

:24 In both faiths, Jesus embodies a path of submission to God's will. In Surah Al-Baqarah (البقرة سورة), revealed in **624** AD, the **Quran** describes those who are *"submissive to Allah"* (**Quran 2:112**), a term that could describe both Jesus and **Muhammad**, as they both submitted to God in their teachings.

:25 In the **Quran**, Jesus is also seen as one who lived simply and served humanity. He rejected wealth and material gain, a virtue upheld in both Islamic and Christian traditions. "He [Jesus] said, '*Indeed, I am a servant of Allah. He has given me the Scripture and made me a prophet*'" (**Quran 19:30**).

:26 In Surah Al-Baqarah, revealed in **624** AD, we find the verse *"Do not desire what we have bestowed on some of them in preference to others"*

(Quran 2:268), emphasizing contentment with God's provision. This mirrors Jesus' teaching to seek spiritual rather than material wealth.

:27 The **Quran** speaks of Jesus' disciples, or **Hawariyun** (ال حواريون), who helped him spread his message. "When Jesus sensed disbelief among his people, he said, '*Who are my supporters for Allah?' The disciples said, 'We are supporters for Allah'*" **(Quran 3:52)**, revealed around **625** AD.

:28 Jesus' call to discipleship echoes the spirit of brotherhood and community found in Islam. In both faiths, followers are encouraged to support one another in their pursuit of righteousness.

:29 Both Jesus and **Muhammad** established communities founded on mutual respect, compassion, and devotion to God. These communities, whether the early Christians or the first Muslims, share common values and ethical frameworks.

:30 The **Quran**'s portrayal of Jesus upholds his teachings of compassion, humility, and dedication to God, drawing connections that make him a respected prophet in Islam.

:31 In this light, we see that Jesus is not only a bridge between **Christianity** and Islam but a figure honored in both faiths for his wisdom, kindness, and devotion to God. Islam's reverence for Jesus as a prophet affirms the shared spiritual heritage that binds these two faiths in respect and admiration for his legacy.

Chapter 4:
Muhammad's Perspective on the Crucifixion

Chapter 4: Muhammad's Perspective on the Crucifixion

:1 Messiahs, as we explore **Muhammad**'s unique perspective on the crucifixion of Jesus, we must delve into the complex religious dynamics of 7th-century Arabia. The question of whether Jesus was crucified is a pivotal point in differentiating Islamic and Christian teachings. The **Quran** challenges the Christian narrative of the crucifixion, presenting a view that has led to much discussion across both traditions.

:2 According to Christian accounts, the crucifixion took place around **30-33** AD, and it became a foundational event for **Christianity**. The New Testament portrays Jesus' crucifixion as the ultimate sacrifice, an act of divine love for humanity's salvation. By the time the **Quran** was revealed to **Muhammad** from **610** to **632** AD, this view of the crucifixion was firmly established in Christian doctrine.

:3 In contrast, the **Quran** presents an alternative account in Surah An-Nisa (الـ ذساء سورة), revealed in **Medina** around **627** AD. The verse states, *"They did not kill him, nor did they crucify him; but it was made to appear so to them"* (**Quran 4:157**). This passage directly addresses the crucifixion, denying that Jesus was killed or crucified in the manner commonly believed.

:4 For Muslims, this verse affirms that Jesus was not humiliated by crucifixion but was protected by God. Islamic tradition holds that God saved Jesus, preserving his honor and redirecting the appearance of crucifixion. This perspective highlights a compassionate and just deity, who intervened to prevent his beloved prophet's suffering.

:5 Early Muslim scholars interpreted this verse in various ways. Some believed that another person, perhaps one of Jesus' followers, was made to resemble him and was crucified in his place. Others viewed it as a metaphorical statement, emphasizing Jesus' spiritual triumph over his enemies rather than a literal escape.

:6 While Islam's account differs from the Gospels, the respect for Jesus' mission remains central. By asserting that Jesus was not crucified, Islam emphasizes that God's chosen messengers are honored and protected, underscoring the divine respect afforded to prophets.

:7 This view contrasts with the accounts in the Gospels, which were composed between **50** and **100** AD. These texts, particularly the accounts in Matthew, Mark, Luke, and John, detail Jesus' suffering, crucifixion, and resurrection, portraying it as a fulfillment of divine prophecy.

:8 Islamic tradition respects Jesus without attributing divinity to him. This perspective aligns with **Muhammad**'s message of strict monotheism: that worship is due to God alone. By rejecting the crucifixion and resurrection narrative, **Muhammad** upheld the principle that God alone is eternal and unchallenged.

:9 Interestingly, despite this rejection, the **Quran**'s depiction of Jesus as the Messiah resonates with the Christian idea of his special mission. The term "Messiah" (المسيح) appears in **Quran 4:171**, asserting Jesus' anointed role. However, Islam interprets this title in a non-divine context, viewing Jesus as a savior figure for his time, sent to guide the Children of Israel.

:10 Another reference to Jesus' unique role is found in Surah Al-Imran (سورة آل عمران), revealed around **625** AD, where Jesus is described as a *"word from God"* (**Quran 3:45**). This title highlights his special creation and mission without implying divinity, bridging a gap of understanding between Islamic and Christian perspectives.

:11 The **Quran**ic interpretation of Jesus as a prophet aligns with **Muhammad**'s larger mission to restore the message of monotheism. **Muhammad** saw himself as a continuation of the prophetic tradition, emphasizing worship of one God and moral guidance over ritual sacrifice or martyrdom.

:12 **Muhammad**'s perspective on Jesus reflects his reverence for previous prophets. In his teachings, **Muhammad** spoke highly of Jesus, viewing him as an esteemed predecessor. This respect is evident in various hadith (أحاديث), sayings of **Muhammad**, which affirm the significance of Jesus.

:13 One notable hadith narrated by Abu Huraira states, *"I am the closest of people to Jesus, the son of Mary, in this life and the Hereafter."* This statement underscores **Muhammad**'s view of Jesus as a brother in faith, a prophet who shares his mission of guiding humanity to God.

:14 The shared values between Jesus and **Muhammad** extend to compassion, charity, and devotion to God. For **Muhammad**, Jesus was a model of purity and humility, ideals he sought to incorporate into his teachings. This connection deepens the bond between Islam and **Christianity**, even amid differing doctrines.

:15 **Muhammad**'s views on Jesus are further clarified in the **Quran**'s account of the Day of Judgment. In Surah Al-Ma'idah (المائدة سورة), revealed around **627** AD, the **Quran** states that Jesus will bear witness to the truth and clarify his teachings: "And on the Day of Resurrection, He will be a witness against them" (**Quran 5:117**).

:16 This belief in Jesus' return aligns with certain Christian doctrines of the Second Coming. In both Islam and **Christianity**, Jesus is expected to fulfill a significant role at the end of times, reinforcing the respect that both faiths hold for him as a prophetic figure.

:17 **Muhammad**'s teachings emphasize the unity of all prophets, recognizing each as a messenger sent by God. Surah Al-Baqarah (سورة البقرة), revealed in **624** AD, underscores this, stating, "We make no distinction between any of His messengers" (**Quran 2:285**). This verse reveals **Muhammad**'s broader mission to affirm all prophets, Jesus included.

:18 **Muhammad**'s rejection of the crucifixion is often seen as an assertion of divine justice. By not allowing Jesus to suffer a humiliating death, God exemplifies mercy, presenting Jesus as an undefeated prophet rather than a martyr.

:19 **Muhammad**'s wife Khadijah and her Christian upbringing also played a role in shaping his early understanding of Jesus and monotheism. As a devout Christian, she supported his prophetic mission and believed in his message, reinforcing the ties between Islam and earlier monotheistic beliefs.

:20 Khadijah's uncle, Waraqah ibn Nawfal, was known as a respected Christian scholar who had memorized the Torah. His knowledge earned him the name "Waraqah" (ورقة), meaning "paper" or "scroll," a testament to his wisdom. Waraqah's faith and his support for **Muhammad** provided an early link between **Muhammad** and the Christian tradition.

:21 According to hadith, after **Muhammad**'s first revelation in **610** AD, Khadijah took him to Waraqah, who recognized **Muhammad**'s experience as prophetic. He reportedly said, "This is the same one who keeps the secrets (Angel Gabriel) whom Allah had sent to Moses." This statement strengthened **Muhammad**'s connection to the monotheistic tradition.

:22 Waraqah's influence underscored the shared heritage of Islam, Judaism, and **Christianity**. His affirmation of **Muhammad** as a prophet reinforced **Muhammad**'s belief that he was part of a long line of messengers, beginning with Adam and including figures like Moses and Jesus.

:23 **Muhammad**'s marriage to Khadijah also reflects the continuity of faith between the Christian and Islamic traditions. Her unwavering support as a devout Christian who believed in his mission highlights the unity of purpose between the two faiths.

:24 Islamic tradition maintains that Khadijah was one of **Muhammad**'s greatest supporters. Her investment in his mission was not only emotional but financial, as she used her wealth to support him and spread his message, much like the early Christian believers who supported Jesus' ministry.

:25 **Muhammad**'s teachings frequently address themes of mercy, justice, and compassion, values he admired in Jesus. The **Quran** reflects these virtues, emphasizing forgiveness, moral integrity, and dedication to God.

:26 Surah Al-Mumtahanah (سورة الممتحنة), revealed around **630** AD, advises Muslims to *"treat with kindness those who do not fight you because* *of religion and do not expel you from your homes"* (**Quran 60:8**). This message of tolerance echoes Jesus' teaching to love one's enemies.

:27 Muhammad's approach to Jesus' life and death emphasizes spiritual strength over physical suffering. The **Quran** depicts Jesus as a figure who, though persecuted, remained steadfast and unbroken—a model for Muslims to emulate in their own lives.

:28 Jesus' crucifixion is replaced in Islam with an emphasis on God's mercy and justice. This distinction sets Islam apart while preserving the respect for Jesus as a prophet who guided others with wisdom and compassion.

:29 The **Quran**'s denial of the crucifixion serves as a reminder that God's plans are not subject to human schemes. Jesus' life, from an Islamic perspective, is seen as divinely protected, highlighting his special status and God's compassion.

:30 Muhammad's reverence for Jesus ultimately reinforces Islam's continuity with earlier monotheistic traditions. His teachings honor Jesus without adopting the crucifixion narrative, creating a balanced respect for Jesus' mission.

:31 In this way, we see **Muhammad**'s perspective on the crucifixion as a unique interpretation that affirms the sanctity of Jesus while maintaining Islam's theological stance. His respect for Jesus illustrates the shared ethical and spiritual heritage between Islam and **Christianity**, despite differences in doctrine.

Chapter 5:
Muhammad's Relationship with Khadijah and Waraqah: The Christian Influence

Chapter 5: Muhammad's Relationship with Khadijah and Waraqah: The Christian Influence

:1 Messiahs, as we look deeper into **Muhammad**'s life, we find that his relationship with his first wife, **Khadijah bint Khuwaylid** (خويلد بنت خديجة), and her Christian uncle, Waraqah ibn Nawfal (نوفل بن ورقة), profoundly shaped his early mission and understanding of monotheism. Khadijah was not only his wife but his steadfast supporter, investor, and spiritual ally, and her devout Christian background played a vital role in his formative years.

:2 Khadijah, a wealthy and respected businesswoman in **Mecca**, was known for her wisdom and integrity. She was a devout Christian, deeply influenced by her faith, and her values aligned with the moral teachings of Jesus. Khadijah's marriage to **Muhammad** was not only a union of love but also of shared spiritual values and purpose.

:3 When **Muhammad** first began receiving revelations in **610** AD, it was Khadijah who provided him with reassurance and confidence. Islamic sources, including early hadith, emphasize her belief in him, seeing him as a true prophet chosen by God. Her Christian faith likely helped her recognize the signs of prophetic calling, encouraging her to support him wholeheartedly.

:4 Khadijah's uncle, **Waraqah ibn Nawfal,** was a Christian scholar renowned for his knowledge of the Torah and the Gospels. His name, "Waraqah," meaning "paper" or "scroll," highlighted his expertise in scripture. Waraqah's dedication to studying religious texts made him a significant figure, well-respected in **Mecca**n society for his wisdom and devotion.

:5 When **Muhammad** experienced his first revelation in the Cave of Hira, he was overwhelmed and fearful, uncertain of what he had encountered. Khadijah, understanding the spiritual nature of his experience, took him to Waraqah for guidance. This moment marked the beginning of **Muhammad**'s journey, where Christian influences became intertwined with his understanding of divine calling.

:6 Waraqah listened intently to **Muhammad**'s account of the angelic visitation. According to a hadith narrated by Aisha, Waraqah immediately recognized the angel Gabriel (جبريل), who had also visited Moses. Waraqah then proclaimed, *"This is the same one who keeps the secrets, whom Allah had sent to Moses"* (**Sahih al-Bukhari,** Book 1, Hadith 3). His words affirmed **Muhammad**'s prophetic experience, grounding it in the tradition of monotheistic prophets.

:7 This recognition by Waraqah was crucial. Not only did it validate **Muhammad**'s experience, but it also aligned his mission with the lineage of earlier prophets from the Jewish and Christian traditions. Waraqah's confirmation reinforced the idea that **Muhammad** was a successor to figures like Moses and Jesus.

:8 Khadijah's faith in **Muhammad** extended beyond mere belief; she invested her wealth and resources to support his mission. She used her influence and financial means to protect him from persecution and ensure that his message could spread. Her support was essential, especially in the early years when **Muhammad**'s followers were few and vulnerable.

:9 Islamic tradition holds that Khadijah's devotion was instrumental in enabling **Muhammad** to pursue his calling. She was often referred to as the first believer (الـمؤمـنـين أول) in Islam, a testament to her unwavering trust in his prophetic mission and her commitment to monotheism.

:10 Khadijah's Christian background likely influenced her perspective, seeing **Muhammad**'s message as a continuation of the teachings of Jesus. Her understanding of Jesus' values—charity, humility, compassion—were virtues that she encouraged **Muhammad** to embody and promote in his revelations.

:11 The influence of Waraqah's Christian knowledge can be observed in certain **Quran**ic passages that reference figures and concepts from the Bible. The **Quran** speaks of Jesus (ع يـسى), Moses (مو سى), and Mary (مريـم) with reverence, presenting them as part of a prophetic lineage that aligns with Waraqah's own beliefs.

:12 In Surah Maryam (مريـم سورة), revealed around **615** AD in **Mecca**, the **Quran** recounts the story of Mary and the miraculous birth of Jesus. This chapter reflects the Christian reverence for Mary, and it may have been inspired, in part, by the stories **Muhammad** learned from Waraqah and Khadijah.

:13 Khadijah's influence extended beyond moral support; her devotion to Christian values helped shape **Muhammad**'s understanding of monotheism and morality. Her unwavering belief that **Muhammad** was chosen by God provided him with the confidence to pursue his message amid adversity.

:14 Waraqah's profound knowledge of scripture also exposed **Muhammad** to the stories and teachings of the prophets in the Torah and the Gospels. His scholarly background provided a theological foundation that **Muhammad** would carry forward into his own revelations.

:15 The **Quran**'s teachings on compassion, mercy, and forgiveness reflect themes common in Christian doctrine, and Waraqah's influence can be seen here. For example, the **Quran**ic emphasis on charity, embodied in the concept of zakat (الزكاة), aligns with Christian values of generosity and care for the less fortunate.

:16 In Surah **Al-Baqarah** (سورة البقرة), revealed around **624** AD, the **Quran** calls for acts of charity, saying, *"Who will lend Allah a good loan which He will multiply for him many times over?"* (**Quran 2:245**). This notion of selfless giving mirrors the Christian emphasis on charity, which Khadijah would have valued deeply.

:17 Khadijah's willingness to sacrifice her wealth for **Muhammad**'s mission illustrates her commitment to both her Christian values and her faith in him. She saw in **Muhammad**'s message an extension of her own beliefs, reinforcing her dedication to his calling.

:18 Waraqah's impact is further seen in the **Quran**'s portrayal of Jesus. In Surah Al-Imran (سورة آل عمران), revealed in **625** AD, Jesus is called a "word from God" (كلمة من الله) and is honored as a prophet. This language reflects a familiarity with Christian teachings that Waraqah would have shared with **Muhammad**.

:19 This verse, "Indeed, the example of Jesus to Allah is like that of Adam. He created him from dust; then He said to him, 'Be,' and he was" (**Quran 3:59**), emphasizes Jesus' unique creation, akin to Christian reverence for his divine mission. Waraqah's influence may have guided **Muhammad**'s respectful yet non-divine portrayal of Jesus.

:20 The reverence shown to Mary in the **Quran** is another indication of the Christian influence in **Muhammad**'s life. Surah Maryam, dedicated entirely to her story, was likely inspired by the respect Khadijah and Waraqah held for Mary. The **Quran**'s emphasis on Mary's purity and devotion mirrors Christian views of her.

:21 Waraqah's presence provided **Muhammad** with a living connection to the traditions of the Torah and the Gospels, grounding his early mission in a shared monotheistic heritage. **Muhammad**'s reverence for Jesus and Moses can be traced, in part, to Waraqah's mentorship.

:22 Islamic sources indicate that Waraqah continued to support **Muhammad** until his passing, shortly after **Muhammad**'s revelations began. His early encouragement left an enduring mark, helping shape **Muhammad**'s understanding of prophetic duty and monotheistic faith.

:23 Khadijah's steadfast support, combined with Waraqah's theological guidance, gave **Muhammad** the foundation he needed to begin his mission with confidence. Their influence bridged the gap between Christian and Islamic beliefs, emphasizing the values that both traditions held sacred.

:24 Hadith sources highlight Khadijah's role as a trusted confidante and believer. She once told **Muhammad**, "God will not disgrace you," affirming her faith in his integrity and divine purpose. Her words reflect her Christian upbringing, as she saw **Muhammad**'s message as aligning with her own spiritual beliefs.

:25 Khadijah's support of **Muhammad** was not only emotional but material. She dedicated her wealth to his cause, believing that his message carried forward the principles she valued. Her role in Islam's early development cannot be understated; she was both a believer and a benefactor.

:26 Islamic tradition reveres Khadijah as the "Mother of the Believers" (أم المؤمنين), a title that acknowledges her foundational role in the Islamic community. Her Christian faith and moral integrity were instrumental in shaping the values that **Muhammad** would later preach.

:27 Waraqah's early endorsement of **Muhammad**'s prophetic mission further legitimized his role as a messenger. His recognition of Gabriel's presence in **Muhammad**'s life linked the new revelation to the long-standing tradition of prophecy, bridging **Christianity** and Islam.

:28 The **Quran**ic stories of Jesus and Mary, along with themes of charity, mercy, and monotheism, reflect the values that Khadijah and Waraqah brought into **Muhammad**'s life. These Christian influences were woven into the **Quran**ic narrative, highlighting shared beliefs.

:29 Khadijah's Christian devotion, combined with Waraqah's knowledge, provided **Muhammad** with a sense of purpose that transcended individual faiths. Together, they helped him see himself as part of a larger tradition of prophets and believers.

:30 As **Muhammad**'s mission evolved, the early Christian influence in his life continued to resonate. His teachings on charity, humility, and justice align with values he shared with Khadijah and Waraqah, reflecting a continuity that bridges Islam with Christian ideals.

:31 Through Khadijah and Waraqah, **Muhammad** found the support, wisdom, and encouragement to carry forth a message that honored the monotheistic traditions of the past while forging a path for the future. Their influence shaped his life, giving Islam a foundation grounded in shared principles and a commitment to God's guidance.

Chapter 6:
Historical Interactions Between Christians and Muslims

Chapter 6: Historical Interactions Between Christians and Muslims

:1 Messiahs, as we proceed, let's examine the early interactions between Christians and Muslims. These encounters, often rooted in mutual respect, demonstrate the shared moral and spiritual values that shaped Islam's development. From the migration to Abyssinia to alliances with Christian tribes, **Muhammad**'s relationship with Christians reveals an appreciation for the teachings of Jesus and a commitment to harmony among the People of the Book.

:2 Around **615** AD, as persecution of the early Muslims intensified in **Mecca**, **Muhammad** advised some of his followers to seek refuge in Abyssinia (modern-day Ethiopia). This migration, known as the Hijrah to Abyssinia, marked one of the first major interactions between Muslims and Christians.

:3 Abyssinia, ruled by the Christian king Negus (الـ نجا شي), was known for its adherence to Christian principles of mercy and compassion. **Muhammad** believed that his followers would find protection under Negus, given the shared values between Islam and **Christianity**.

:4 According to Islamic tradition, when the Muslim refugees reached Abyssinia, they were welcomed by Negus. He offered them sanctuary, listening attentively to their account of **Muhammad**'s message. This act of kindness highlights the early respect between the two faiths, rooted in mutual compassion and respect for monotheism.

:5 During their stay, the **Mecca**n leaders attempted to sway Negus against the Muslims, accusing them of abandoning their ancestral beliefs. In response, Negus invited the Muslim refugees to explain their faith, allowing them to share the teachings of **Muhammad** openly.

:6 The delegation of Muslims, led by Ja'far ibn Abi Talib (أبـ ي بـ ن جـ ع فر طالـ ب), recited verses from Surah Maryam (مريـ م سورة), including passages that honor Mary and Jesus. Moved by the **Quran**'s reverence for these figures, Negus is reported to have said, "This and what Jesus brought have come from the same source."

:7 This moment underscored the spiritual connection between Islam and **Christianity**. By acknowledging the **Quran**'s reverence for Jesus and Mary, Negus recognized **Muhammad**'s message as aligned with Christian values, further affirming the shared respect between the two faiths.

:8 Islamic tradition holds that Negus accepted Islam, though he did not formally convert. His support for the Muslim refugees reflects his recognition of Islam's connection to **Christianity**, emphasizing the shared monotheistic heritage that unites both faiths.

:9 The Hijrah to Abyssinia not only protected the early Muslims but also established a precedent of respect between Christians and Muslims. This early encounter laid a foundation for peaceful coexistence, demonstrating **Muhammad**'s vision for harmony among the People of the Book.

:10 Another significant encounter occurred with the Christian Arab tribe of Najran, located in present-day Saudi Arabia. The Christians of Najran were known for their devotion and knowledge of the Gospels, practicing a form of **Christianity** influenced by early Eastern traditions.

:11 In **630** AD, the Christians of Najran sent a delegation to **Medina** to engage with **Muhammad**. This meeting marked one of the first diplomatic exchanges between Muslims and Christians, underscoring a mutual willingness to understand and respect each other's beliefs.

:12 During their stay, the delegation was welcomed into **Muhammad**'s mosque, where they were even permitted to perform their Christian prayers. This gesture of hospitality and religious tolerance exemplifies **Muhammad**'s respect for religious diversity and his commitment to peaceful relations.

:13 The exchange between **Muhammad** and the Najran Christians culminated in the signing of a treaty, granting the Christians religious freedom and protection in exchange for their allegiance to the Muslim state.

This treaty became a model for future interactions between Muslims and non-Muslims.

:14 The **Quran** acknowledges Christians as "People of the Book" (أهل الكتاب), a term that recognizes their shared belief in divine revelation. Surah Al-Ma'idah (سورة المائدة), revealed around **627** AD, states, "Indeed, the believers, Jews, **Sabians,** and Christians—whoever believes in Allah and the Last Day and does righteousness—no fear will there be concerning them" (**Quran 5:69**).

:15 This verse highlights the **Quran**'s inclusive vision, affirming that righteousness and belief in God form the basis of salvation. **Muhammad**'s respect for the People of the Book reflects his view that Islam continues the monotheistic tradition established by prophets like Moses and Jesus.

:16 Muhammad's interactions with Christians were not only respectful but often protective. In **631** AD, he sent a letter to the monks of St. Catherine's Monastery in Sinai, offering them his protection. The letter, known as the *Ashtiname of **Muhammad*** (محمد النبي عهد), guarantees safety to Christians under Muslim rule.

:17 The *Ashtiname* states, "No one is to destroy a house of their religion, to damage it, or to carry anything from it to the Muslims' houses." This document stands as a testament to **Muhammad**'s commitment to safeguarding Christian communities, reinforcing his respect for their beliefs and places of worship.

:18 Islamic sources, including hadith, highlight **Muhammad**'s respect for Christians. One well-known hadith narrated by Abu Dawood states, "Whoever wrongs a person with whom a treaty has been made… *I will be his opponent on the Day of Judgment."* This saying reflects **Muhammad**'s dedication to justice and fair treatment of non-Muslim communities.

:19 Muhammad's emphasis on justice extended to economic and social relations as well. In treaties with Christian tribes, he granted them autonomy in exchange for a tax called **jizya** (الـ جزـية), allowing them to practice their faith freely while contributing to the protection of the Muslim state.

:20 The **jizya** was not merely a financial obligation; it represented a pact of mutual protection. In return for the tax, Muslim authorities promised to protect the rights and safety of Christian communities, creating a model of coexistence that balanced responsibility with respect.

:21 Historical records show that Christians, particularly in the Levant and North Africa, often preferred Muslim rule over the **Byzantine Empire**. The Byzantine authorities imposed religious uniformity, whereas Muslim rulers allowed greater religious freedom, respecting Christian practices.

:22 Under **Muhammad**'s leadership, the early Muslim state was known for its tolerance and fair treatment of religious minorities. This respect fostered trust among Christians, creating alliances that strengthened the Muslim community and promoted peaceful coexistence.

:23 **Muhammad**'s interactions with Christians reflect his vision of a society built on shared values of compassion, justice, and monotheism. He saw Christians as part of the broader monotheistic tradition, emphasizing the common moral teachings between Islam and **Christianity**.

:24 The **Quran** further emphasizes the closeness between Muslims and Christians. Surah Al-Ma'idah, revealed in **627** AD, states, "You will find the nearest of them in affection to the believers those who say, 'We are Christians.' *That is because among them are priests and monks, and they are not arrogant*" (**Quran 5:82**).

:25 This verse highlights the **Quran**'s acknowledgment of Christian humility and devotion, attributes that align with Islamic values. **Muhammad**'s interactions with Christians reflect this mutual respect, creating bonds based on shared reverence for God.

:26 Historical sources indicate that **Muhammad**'s respectful treatment of Christians influenced his followers, who continued this tradition. Later

Islamic leaders, including the caliphs, upheld treaties with Christian communities, maintaining **Muhammad**'s legacy of tolerance.

:27 **Muhammad**'s encounters with Christian communities demonstrate that his mission was not about conversion but about fostering harmony and understanding. By respecting Christian practices, he encouraged mutual respect and coexistence, aligning with the teachings of Jesus on love and tolerance.

:28 The early Muslim-Christian alliances served as a foundation for future relations between the two faiths. **Muhammad**'s diplomatic and compassionate approach set a precedent that would shape Islamic governance and interfaith relations for centuries.

:29 Islamic tradition records **Muhammad**'s admiration for the Christian ethics of charity, humility, and forgiveness. His interactions with Christians reinforced these shared values, affirming the moral alignment between the teachings of Jesus and Islam.

:30 The respectful interactions between **Muhammad** and Christian communities reveal a deep sense of kinship. Islam recognizes **Christianity**'s contributions to monotheism, emphasizing the common values that unite these two faiths.

:31 Through these interactions, we see **Muhammad**'s commitment to unity and peace, grounded in the shared principles of justice, mercy, and devotion to God. His respect for Christians reflects a vision of harmony among the People of the Book, showing that, while distinct, these faiths are connected by their pursuit of truth and righteousness.

Chapter 7:
Influence of Popes and Rulers on the Development of Islam

Chapter 7: Influence of Popes and Rulers on the Development of Islam

:1 Messiahs, in this chapter, we examine the influence of various Christian popes and rulers on the historical development of Islam. Through political alliances, cultural exchanges, and theological debates, the interplay between Christian and Muslim leaders shaped the trajectory of both faiths. Understanding these relationships sheds light on how certain elements within **Christianity** left an imprint on Islam.

:2 By the time of **Muhammad**'s prophethood in the **7**th century, **Christianity** had already spread throughout the **Byzantine Empire**. The Eastern Roman Empire, or **Byzantine Empire**, was a Christian stronghold, and its leaders, including the popes and emperors, wielded significant religious and political influence.

:3 The Byzantine Emperor **Heraclius,** who reigned from **610** to **641** AD, played a notable role in the early history of Islam. Heraclius, known for his campaigns against the Sassanian Empire, had an extensive interaction with the Arabian Peninsula, where **Muhammad**'s influence was growing.

:4 In **628** AD, **Muhammad** sent letters to several world leaders, including Heraclius, inviting them to accept Islam. According to historical sources, Heraclius responded with diplomatic respect, viewing **Muhammad** as a legitimate leader and recognizing the shared monotheistic beliefs.

:5 The correspondence between **Muhammad** and Heraclius is preserved in Islamic tradition, where it is said that Heraclius saw **Muhammad** as a prophetic figure. Although he did not convert, Heraclius respected Islam, recognizing the values it shared with **Christianity**.

a

:6 Pope Honorius I, who served as the Pope of Rome from **625** to **638** AD, held similar stance. Though there is no direct record of correspondence between Honorius and **Muhammad**, the Pope's contemporaneous theological debates over monotheism and the nature of Christ may have indirectly influenced Islamic teachings on strict monotheism.

:7 The **Council of Chalcedon** in **451** AD, which addressed the nature of Christ, highlighted theological rifts within **Christianity**, particularly over the divinity and humanity of Jesus. These debates influenced early Islamic views, where **Muhammad** upheld the concept of Jesus as a prophet, rejecting his divinity but honoring his moral teachings.

:8 The Christian rejection of icon worship also resonated with **Muhammad**'s teachings. Islam strictly forbids images of God, aligning with certain Christian sects, like the Iconoclasts, who opposed the veneration of icons and religious images.

:9 The **Byzantine Empire**'s use of religious councils, such as the Council of Nicaea in **325** AD, set a precedent for theological debate and dogma. Although Islam formed independently, **Muhammad**'s emphasis on strict monotheism echoed these early Christian efforts to define a unified belief system.

:10 Another influential figure was **Pope Sergius** I, who served from **687** to **701** AD, shortly after **Muhammad**'s time. Pope **Sergius** was known for his efforts to reconcile the theological conflicts that persisted within **Christianity**, and his teachings on monotheism likely resonated with Islamic perspectives.

:11 During the rise of Islam, Christian theological schools in Alexandria, Antioch, and Jerusalem contributed to the intellectual climate of the region. These centers fostered religious scholarship, and their discussions on monotheism and ethics paralleled early Islamic teachings.

:12 The Christian presence in Alexandria, known for its theological debates on God's nature, created a context in which **Muhammad**'s message of tawhid (تَوْحِيد), or absolute monotheism, would find both resonance and distinction.

:13 Political alliances between Christian and Muslim leaders also influenced the development of Islam. For example, the Christian Arab Ghassanid tribe allied with the **Byzantine Empire**, creating an environment where Arabs were exposed to Christian doctrines, possibly shaping early Islamic values.

:14 The Ghassanids were monophysite Christians, a sect that emphasized the singular divine nature of Christ. This belief, distinct from the Byzantine orthodoxy, may have influenced **Muhammad**'s conception of Jesus as a prophet, rather than as a divine figure.

:15 Furthermore, the Christian Kingdom of Aksum, across the Red Sea in Ethiopia, played a role in protecting early Muslims. King Negus of Aksum, a devout Christian, granted asylum to the Muslim refugees who fled **Mecca** in **615** AD, demonstrating the early alliance between Christians and Muslims.

:16 This refuge in Aksum was a formative experience for early Muslims, reinforcing the respect **Muhammad** had for Christians as People of the Book. The mutual tolerance between King Negus and **Muhammad**'s followers set a precedent for interfaith diplomacy.

:17 Historical records show that Islamic scholars were also influenced by Christian philosophers. In the Abbasid era (**750–1258** AD), Islamic scholars translated Greek and Syriac works on philosophy and medicine, many of which were preserved by Christian scholars.

:18 Figures like **Al-Kindi,** known as the "Philosopher of the Arabs," studied Greek philosophy through Christian sources, merging Hellenistic thought with Islamic teachings. These exchanges enriched Islamic philosophy, showing the impact of Christian intellectual contributions.

:19 In addition to intellectual influences, Christian rulers sometimes sought alliances with Muslim leaders for political reasons. During the early Umayyad period, Byzantine-Muslim relations fluctuated between conflict and cooperation, depending on the needs of the time.

:20 By the **8**th century, Islamic Spain became a center for religious and cultural exchange. Christians, Jews, and Muslims coexisted in cities like Cordoba, where philosophical and scientific knowledge flourished. The influence of Christian scholarship and theology can be seen in the works of Muslim philosophers in Spain.

:21 Another prominent example of Christian influence on Islam is the Dome of the Rock, completed in **691** AD in Jerusalem. Commissioned by the Umayyad Caliph Abd al-Malik, the Dome reflects Byzantine

architectural styles, blending Christian and Islamic aesthetics.

:22 The Dome of the Rock's inscriptions also emphasize the oneness of God, countering Christian doctrines of the Trinity. These inscriptions reflect the Islamic stance on monotheism while acknowledging the theological debates between **Christianity** and Islam.

:23 Throughout history, interactions between Christian and Muslim leaders often involved theological discussions. Some Byzantine emperors and popes recognized the **Quran**'s respect for Jesus and Mary, and Islamic leaders reciprocated by showing respect for Christian teachings.

:24 In the **9**th century, Caliph Al-Mamun established the House of Wisdom in Baghdad, where Muslim and Christian scholars worked together to translate and study Greek, Syriac, and Latin texts. This collaboration fostered mutual respect and intellectual growth.

:25 Christian monastic communities also had an impact on Islamic teachings on asceticism and piety. The **Quran**'s emphasis on humility, charity, and dedication to God aligns with the monastic values practiced by early Christian monks.

:26 Surah Al-Hadid (سورة ال حدي د), revealed in **628** AD, praises asceticism, stating, *"And We placed in the hearts of those who followed him compassion* *and mercy. But monasticism they invented, which We did not prescribe for them"* (**Quran 57:27**). This verse acknowledges Christian monasticism while emphasizing balance.

:27 The translation movement in the Abbasid era led to the incorporation of Christian, Greek, and Persian knowledge into Islamic culture. Christian scholars preserved much of this knowledge, allowing Islamic thinkers to draw from a rich intellectual tradition.

:28 Christian physicians, especially those in the Nestorian community, contributed to Islamic medical knowledge. Nestorian Christians, who preserved Greek medical texts, served in the courts of Abbasid caliphs, blending medical practices across faiths.

:29 Pope Urban II's call for the First Crusade in **1095** AD marked a turbulent era in Christian-Muslim relations. However, even during the Crusades, moments of mutual respect and exchanges of knowledge persisted between Christian and Muslim leaders.

:30 Christian and Muslim leaders continued to influence each other through cultural and intellectual exchanges, even amid political conflicts. These interactions shaped the theological and philosophical developments of both faiths.

:31 Through these relationships, Islam and **Christianity** engaged in a dynamic exchange of ideas, values, and knowledge. While maintaining distinct beliefs, the influence of Christian rulers, popes, and scholars enriched Islamic thought, reinforcing the connections between these two great traditions.

Chapter 8:
The Spread of Islam and the Message of Jesus

Chapter 8: The Spread of Islam and the Message of Jesus

:1 Messiahs, as we continue this journey, let us examine how Islam spread its message of monotheism, justice, and compassion, and how these principles echoed the teachings of Jesus. The early spread of Islam was marked by a focus on social justice, charity, and reverence for God, principles that resonated with Christian communities and contributed to Islam's rapid expansion.

:2 Islam's message of universal brotherhood and equality struck a chord with the people of Arabia and beyond. **Muhammad**'s mission emphasized the oneness of humanity under God, a teaching similar to Jesus' call to love one's neighbor as oneself (Matthew **22:39**), spoken around **30** AD. This shared ethic fostered common ground between the two faiths.

:3 **Muhammad**'s teachings on charity, or zakat (الزكاة), became a cornerstone of the Muslim faith. Instituted as one of the Five Pillars of Islam in **622** AD, zakat calls for Muslims to give a portion of their wealth to the needy. This principle of charity mirrors Jesus' teachings, such as in the Gospel of Matthew, where he urges generosity toward the poor (Matthew **19:21**).

:4 As Islam spread across the Arabian Peninsula, the emphasis on social welfare and support for the vulnerable was appealing to those who had been marginalized. **Muhammad**'s message was not solely religious but also social, focusing on uplifting the oppressed and emphasizing moral conduct.

:5 The **Quran** frequently calls for believers to treat others with compassion and respect. In Surah Al-Mumtahanah (سورة الممتحنة), revealed around **630** AD, God commands, *"Allah does not forbid you from those who do not fight you because of religion and do not expel you from your homes—from being righteous toward them and acting justly toward them"* (**Quran 60:8**). This respect for peaceful coexistence aligns with Jesus' teachings on tolerance and love.

:**6** Islam's early expansion was marked by alliances with neighboring communities, including Christian and Jewish tribes. These alliances fostered peaceful relations and demonstrated **Muhammad**'s respect for the People of the Book. This interfaith cooperation allowed Islam's ethical and spiritual message to reach a broader audience.

:**7** As Islam expanded, **Muhammad** and his successors established treaties with Christian communities that granted them religious freedom and protection in exchange for loyalty. These agreements, like the treaty with the Christians of Najran, set a precedent for mutual respect and peaceful coexistence.

:**8** The spread of Islam into regions like Syria, Palestine, and Egypt introduced Christian communities to Islamic teachings on monotheism and moral behavior. Many of these communities found common values in the ethical teachings of both Jesus and **Muhammad**, leading to a more harmonious integration.

:**9** Islamic tradition holds that Jesus' teachings on mercy and forgiveness inspired the Muslim approach to social justice. In the **Quran**, God states, *"And My Mercy encompasses all things"* (**Quran 7:156**), a principle that guided Islamic governance, encouraging rulers to be merciful and just.

:**10** As Islam continued to grow, it incorporated Christian ideals of humility and service. **Muhammad**'s emphasis on humility before God was reflected in the **Quran**ic call to avoid pride and arrogance. This value aligns with Jesus' teaching, *"Blessed are the meek, for they shall inherit the earth"* (**Matthew 5:5),** written around **80–90** AD.

:**11** Islam's spread was not achieved solely by military conquest but through the appeal of its ethical teachings. Merchants, scholars, and diplomats carried Islam's message of compassion and justice into Africa, Persia, and Asia, creating communities founded on shared values.

:**12** Christian communities in North Africa and the Levant often viewed Islamic rule as more tolerant than Byzantine rule. Islamic governance allowed Christians to practice their faith, a contrast to the strict doctrinal enforcement of the **Byzantine Empire**.

:13 This tolerance created an environment where Islam could coexist with **Christianity**, fostering a cultural exchange that enriched both faiths. Christian and Muslim scholars studied together, sharing knowledge in fields like philosophy, medicine, and theology.

:14 The Islamic concept of ummah (أمة), or community, emphasized unity and cooperation among believers. This idea of a unified community under God resonated with Christian teachings on the body of believers, where Jesus spoke of his followers as one body (**1** Corinthians **12:12**), a metaphor that reflected unity.

:15 As Islam spread, it maintained respect for Jesus and Mary. The **Quran** honors both figures, describing Jesus as a prophet and Mary as a woman of purity. This reverence for Christian figures helped create a sense of connection between the two faiths.

:16 The **Quran**'s emphasis on Jesus as a prophet who preached compassion and humility influenced the way early Muslims viewed **Christianity**. Islamic sources respect Jesus' teachings, particularly his calls for social justice and mercy, values that aligned with Islamic principles.

:17 **Muhammad**'s example of interfaith respect shaped the early Islamic state's policies toward Christians. The protection of Christian communities under Islamic rule allowed Islam to spread without forcing conversions, creating a model of coexistence that was both practical and ethical.

:18 As Islam spread to Persia, the Christian communities there found Islamic rule to be accommodating, allowing them to continue their religious practices. This tolerance fostered a sense of security and respect, encouraging the spread of Islam through peaceful means.

:19 The **Quran** also contains stories that resonate with Christian parables, such as those that emphasize humility, charity, and trust in God. These narratives helped Christians relate to Islam's message, reinforcing the shared ethical foundation between the two religions.

:20 The ethical teachings in both the **Quran** and the New Testament promoted values of kindness, honesty, and respect for others. This shared moral code allowed Islam's message to find common ground with **Christianity**, facilitating its spread among Christian communities.

:21 Muslim conquests were often followed by policies that allowed religious freedom, a stark contrast to the forced conversions seen in other empires. This approach helped Islam establish itself in diverse regions without alienating local populations.

:22 Islamic rule in Spain, particularly during the **Umayyad period,** created a vibrant culture where Muslims, Christians, and Jews coexisted. This period of convivencia, or coexistence, allowed the values of Islam to be  shared and appreciated across religious boundaries.

:23 The teachings of Jesus on forgiveness and reconciliation were mirrored in the **Quran**'s guidance on dealing with others. In Surah Ash-Shura (سورة الـ شورى), revealed around **620** AD, God states, *"The reward for an injury is an injury equal thereto; but if a person forgives and makes reconciliation, his reward is due from Allah"* (**Quran 42:40**).

:24 This emphasis on forgiveness strengthened Islam's message of mercy, encouraging Muslims to adopt a spirit of forgiveness that aligned with Jesus' teachings. This shared ethic contributed to Islam's appeal among Christian communities.

:25 As Islam spread into regions like the Caucasus, the Balkans, and Central Asia, it adapted to local cultures while maintaining its core principles of faith, justice, and charity. This adaptability helped Islam resonate with diverse populations, including Christian communities.

:26 **Muhammad**'s respect for the teachings of Jesus and his emphasis on social justice were key factors in Islam's spread. His vision of a just society, where the poor and marginalized were cared for, echoed Jesus' call for compassion toward the vulnerable.

:27 Islamic teachings on justice and equity appealed to Christian communities that valued similar principles. The **Quran**'s calls for justice and moral integrity created a sense of kinship with the teachings of Jesus, fostering respect for Islamic principles.

:28 Islamic scholars who engaged with Christian theologians often found common ground on issues of ethics and morality. This dialogue allowed for a mutual exchange of ideas that enriched both Islamic and Christian thought.

:29 As Islam spread across Africa, Asia, and Europe, it left a legacy of cultural exchange with **Christianity**. This interfaith dialogue helped Islam gain acceptance and respect, particularly among Christian communities that valued ethical teachings.

:30 The shared values of compassion, mercy, and humility formed a bridge between Islam and **Christianity**. These common values allowed Islam to expand peacefully, creating a legacy of coexistence and mutual respect between the two faiths.

:31 Through its message of justice, charity, and reverence for God, Islam built on the ethical teachings of Jesus, creating a faith that resonated with diverse communities and allowed for peaceful coexistence with **Christianity**. This harmony of values strengthened Islam's foundation and legacy, uniting it with **Christianity** in a shared vision of faith and compassion.

Conclusion: Reexamining the Legacy of Muhammad as a Christ-Like Figure

Conclusion: Reexamining the Legacy of Muhammad as a Christ-Like Figure

:1 Messiahs, as we bring our exploration to a close, let us reexamine **Muhammad**'s legacy, especially through the lens of his Christ-like qualities. Despite doctrinal differences, **Muhammad** embodied virtues that align with the teachings of Jesus, reinforcing the shared ethical and spiritual heritage of Islam and **Christianity**.

:2 The term "Christian," meaning "Christ-like," denotes one who lives according to the teachings and values that Jesus promoted—compassion, humility, charity, and justice. While **Muhammad** did not identify as Christian, his life and teachings often mirrored these Christ-like values.

:3 **Muhammad**'s focus on monotheism echoes Jesus' teachings on the worship of one God. In the Gospel of John, written around **90** AD, Jesus declares, *"The Lord our God, the Lord is one"* (Mark **12:29**). **Muhammad**'s mission to uphold tawhid (ﺗَﻮﺣِﻴﺪ), or the oneness of God, reflects a similar dedication to monotheism.

:4 The **Quran**ic message, which spans from **610** to **632** AD, consistently emphasizes that God is singular and without partners. This foundation of monotheism is shared by both Islam and **Christianity**, rooted in Jesus' own reverence for the one true God.

:5 **Muhammad**'s life also reflects humility, a virtue deeply valued by Jesus. In his early life as a shepherd and later as a trader, **Muhammad** led a life of modesty, often placing the needs of others above his own, just as Jesus did. This humility earned him respect and trust among the people of **Mecca**.

:6 When **Muhammad** became a leader, he maintained this humility, often reminding his followers that he was a "servant of God." Like Jesus, who washed his disciples' feet to teach humility (John **13:14-15**), **Muhammad** practiced humility in his actions and interactions.

:7 Muhammad's dedication to social justice aligns with Jesus' teachings on compassion for the oppressed. In the Gospel of Luke, written around **80** AD, Jesus says, *"The Spirit of the Lord is upon me…to proclaim good news to the poor"* (Luke **4:18**). **Muhammad**, too, focused on uplifting the marginalized and caring for the vulnerable in society.

:8 The **Quran**ic mandate of zakat (الزکاة), or almsgiving, established around **622** AD, reflects this commitment to social welfare. **Muhammad** instructed his followers to support the needy, embodying the same principles of charity that Jesus preached.

:9 Muhammad's teachings on forgiveness reflect the mercy Jesus promoted. In the Gospel of Matthew, written around **80-90** AD, Jesus teaches, *"Love your enemies and pray for those who persecute you"* (Matthew **5:44**). **Muhammad**, even in times of conflict, showed mercy to his enemies.

:10 The Conquest of **Mecca** in **630** AD provides a profound example of **Muhammad**'s forgiveness. Rather than seeking vengeance against those who had opposed him, he granted a general amnesty, mirroring Jesus' ethic of forgiveness and reconciliation.

:11 Muhammad's respect for the People of the Book reflects his belief in a shared divine mission. He taught his followers to honor Jews and Christians, encouraging peaceful coexistence. This view aligns with Jesus' teaching to *"love your neighbor as yourself"* (Matthew **22:39**).

:12 The **Quran** emphasizes this respect, stating, "You will find the nearest of them in affection to the believers those who say, '*We are Christians*'" (**Quran 5:82**), revealed in **627** AD. **Muhammad**'s respect for Christians reflects his Christ-like regard for those of different faiths.

:13 Muhammad's vision of a community united under God mirrors Jesus' call for unity among his followers. In John **17:21**, Jesus prays "that they all may be one." **Muhammad**, too, called for unity among believers, teaching that all humanity shares a bond as God's creation.

:14 The Islamic concept of **ummah** (أمة), or community, emphasizes mutual support and compassion. This principle reflects Jesus' message of **fellowship** and **collective faith,** building a community bound by love and shared responsibility.

:15 **Muhammad**'s emphasis on forgiveness and patience in the face of hardship resonates with Jesus' teachings. When faced with persecution in **Mecca**, **Muhammad** advised his followers to *"bear patiently what they say and depart from them in peace"* (**Quran 73:10**).

:16 This focus on peaceful endurance aligns with Jesus' counsel to *"turn the other cheek"* (Matthew **5:39**), written around **80-90** AD. Both prophets encouraged patience, showing that spiritual strength lies in restraint and forgiveness.

:17 **Muhammad**'s teachings on humility are exemplified in the **Quran**'s emphasis on avoiding arrogance. In Surah Luqman (لـ قمان سورة), revealed around **615** AD, God says, *"And do not walk upon the earth arrogantly"* (**Quran 31:18**). This counsel echoes Jesus' teaching that "the meek shall inherit the earth" (Matthew **5:5**).

:18 Like Jesus, **Muhammad** warned against materialism and greed. He taught his followers to seek spiritual wealth rather than material gain, advising, *"True richness is the richness of the soul"* (Sahih al-Bukhari). This teaching aligns with Jesus' warning that "one's life does not consist in the abundance of possessions" (Luke **12:15**).

:19 **Muhammad**'s approach to leadership also reflected Jesus' humility. He lived simply, even as a leader, sleeping on a mat and refusing to amass wealth. This modesty recalls Jesus' words, "The Son of Man has no place to lay his head" (Matthew **8:20**).

:20 **Muhammad**'s respect for Mary (مريم) in the **Quran** also demonstrates his reverence for Jesus' legacy. Surah Maryam, revealed in **615** AD, honors Mary's piety and her role as the mother of Jesus, reflecting a respect for Christian figures.

:21 Muhammad's compassion extended to all people, regardless of their faith. He encouraged kindness toward others, echoing Jesus' teaching, "Do to others as you would have them do to you" (Luke **6:31**). This Golden Rule resonates within both Islam and **Christianity**.

:22 Both Jesus and **Muhammad** emphasized the value of family and the duty to honor parents. The **Quran** states, "*And We have enjoined upon man, to his parents, good treatment*" (**Quran 31:14**). Jesus similarly taught to "*honor your father and mother*" (Matthew **19:19**), showing their shared respect for family bonds.

:23 Muhammad's relationship with Khadijah reflects a Christ-like partnership of love and mutual support. Khadijah's devotion to **Muhammad**'s mission, rooted in her own Christian values, was instrumental in shaping his early prophetic journey.

:24 Islamic tradition holds that Khadijah was the first to believe in **Muhammad**'s mission. Her support reflects the same dedication that Jesus' disciples showed him, affirming her role as a believer and guide.

:25 **Muhammad**'s interactions with Christians highlight his Christ-like compassion and respect for other faiths. The *Ashtiname of Muhammad*, a document granting protection to the monks of St. Catherine's Monastery, reflects his respect for Christian communities.

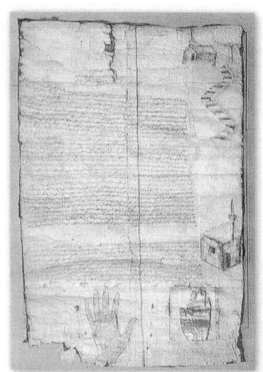

:26 The *Ashtiname* states, "No one is to destroy a house of their religion." This guarantee of protection shows **Muhammad**'s commitment to interfaith respect, a Christ-like gesture of tolerance and peace.

:27 **Muhammad**'s dedication to social reform and justice aligns with Jesus' mission. Both prophets challenged corrupt systems, advocating for the marginalized. **Muhammad**'s teachings on justice reflect the same moral courage that Jesus displayed.

:28 **Muhammad**'s advocacy for equality among people reflects Jesus' teaching that "all are equal in God's sight." **Muhammad**'s message dismantled social hierarchies, emphasizing that one's worth lies in faith and righteousness rather than status.

:29 **Muhammad**'s portrayal of Jesus in the **Quran** as a prophet and servant of God respects Jesus' role in the Abrahamic tradition. Islam honors Jesus, not as divine, but as a model of piety, humility, and obedience to God.

:30 Muhammad's legacy as a Christ-like figure reveals the deep ethical and spiritual connections between Islam and **Christianity**. His commitment to humility, charity, justice, and reverence for God demonstrates the values shared by both faiths.

:31 Through his Christ-like qualities, **Muhammad**'s life and teachings resonate with Jesus' message, revealing a spiritual kinship that binds these two faiths. His legacy invites us to see Islam not as a divergence, but as a continuation of the values Jesus upheld—values of compassion, mercy, and unity under the one God.

747-24-7-361* Qhum, Peace and Salutations to the Messiahs! Contact the Movement *@themessiahcode131@gmail.com* or watch on YouTube
@THEMESSIAHCODE